Contents

What to Do 2

An Idea 4

A Mermaid's Tail 6

A New Fin Tail 8

A New Beak 10

Helping Oscar – A New Idea 12

A Success Story 14

Something to Think About 16

Do You Need to Find an Answer? 18

Do You Want to Find Out More? 19

Word Help 20

Location Help 23

Index 24

What to Do

Choose a face

Remember the colour you have chosen.

When you see your face on the page, you are the LEADER.

The LEADER reads the text in the speech bubbles.

There are extra words and questions to help you on the teacher's whiteboard. The LEADER reads these aloud.

When you see this stop sign, the LEADER reads it aloud.

You might need:

- to look at the WORD HELP on pages 20–22;
- to look at the LOCATION HELP on page 23;
- an atlas.

If you are the LEADER, follow these steps:

1 PREDICT 

Think about what is on the page.

- Say to your group:

"I am looking at this page and I think it is going to be about…"

- Tell your group:

"Read the page to yourselves."

2 CLARIFY 

Talk about words and their meaning.

- Say to your group:

"Are there any words you don't know?"

"Is there anything else on the page you didn't understand?"

- Talk about the words and their meanings with your group.

- Read the whiteboard.

- Ask your group to find the LET'S CHECK word in the WORD HELP on pages 20–22. Ask them to read the meaning of the word aloud.

3 ASK QUESTIONS 

Talk about how to find out more.

- Say to your group:

"Who has a question about what we have read?"

- Question starters are: how…, why…, when…, where…, what…, who…

- Read the question on the whiteboard and talk about it with your group.

4 SUMMARISE 

Think about who and what the story was mainly about.

When you get to pages 16–17, you can talk to a partner or write and draw on your own.

 or 

An Idea

Nadya was just a child when she had a leg **amputated**. Later on, her other leg was amputated, too. Doctors made her **artificial** legs so that she could walk.

Nadya liked to swim, but she had to take off her artificial legs when she did. One day, a small boy asked her why she didn't have any legs. Nadya told him that she was a mermaid.

Nadya's answer to the boy gave her an idea. She could swim like a mermaid, if she had a mermaid's tail.

Let's check: amputated

Why do you think it might be difficult for Nadya to swim without legs?

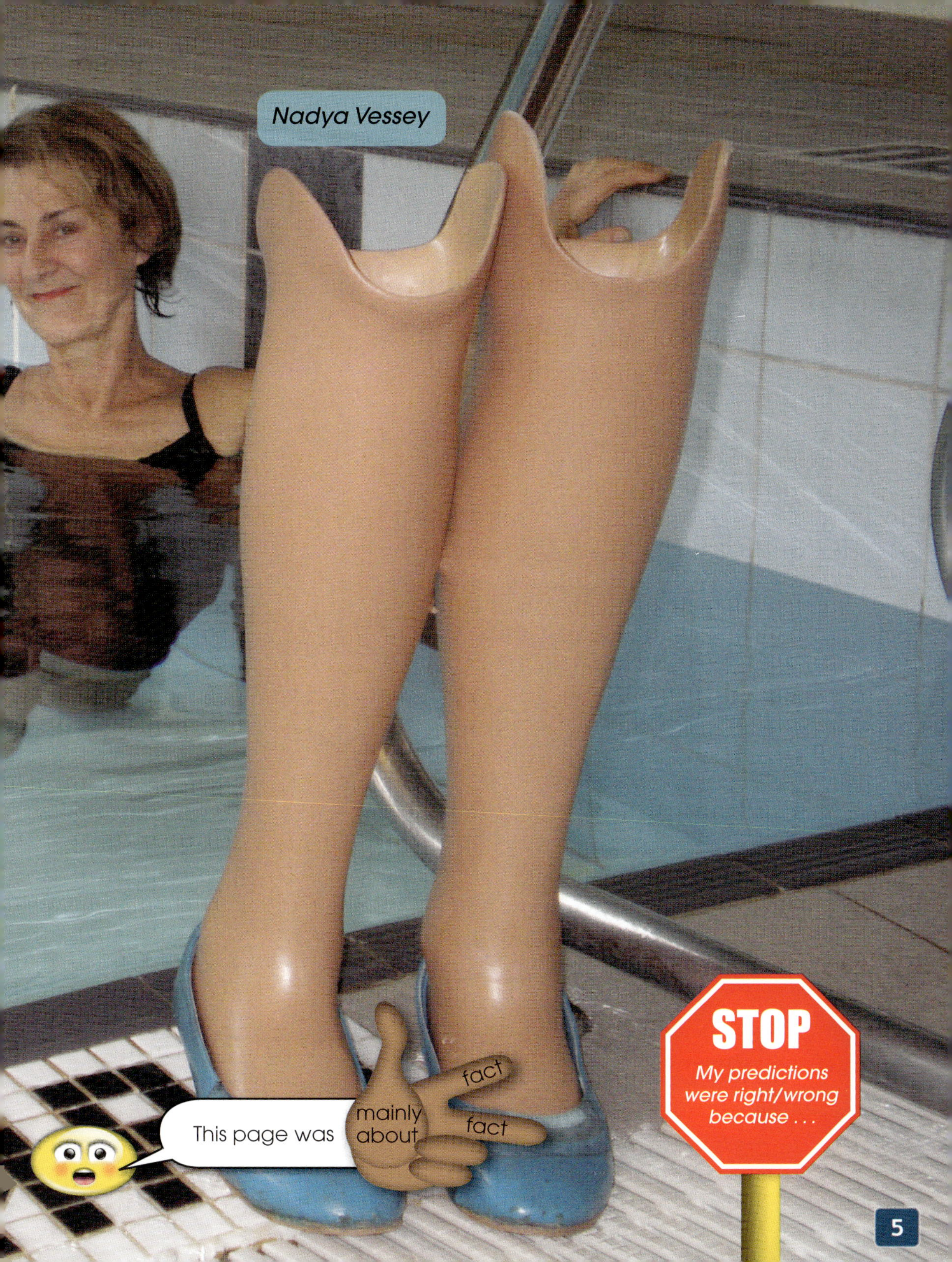
Nadya Vessey
This page was
mainly
about
fact
fact
STOP
My predictions
were right/wrong
because . . .
5

A Mermaid's Tail

Nadya went to Weta Workshop, where creatures for films are made. This was the place that could make a mermaid's tail for her.

The people at Weta Workshop made a **spine** and tail fin from a material that is like strong **plastic**. The skin of the tail was made from **wetsuit** material. Then they printed **scales** on the outside to make it look real.

At first, swimming with a tail was very different for Nadya. But now she can swim like a mermaid.

How do you think that swimming with a tail was different for Nadya?

Nadya swims with her tail fin.
This page was mainly about
fact
fact
STOP
My predictions were right/wrong because . . .
7

A New Fin Tail

Many people have artificial body parts. Now, some animals do too.

Fuji is a dolphin with an artificial tail fin. Fuji's real tail fin had to be amputated because of a **disease**.

Dolphins can't live without a tail fin, so a rubber one was made for her. At first it didn't work, but the people kept trying. Fuji needed a tail fin that was strong and fast. After trying many fins, one was made that worked. Then Fuji could swim and leap again.

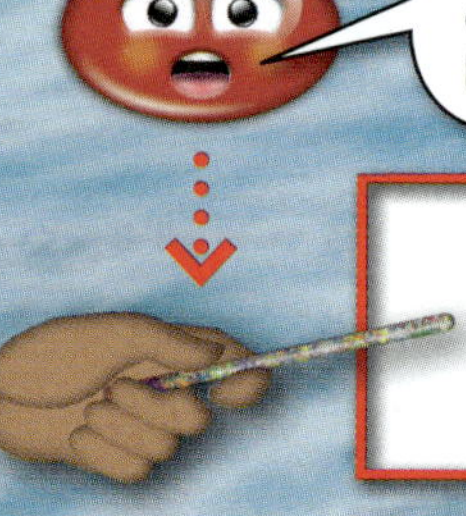

Workers strap a tail fin onto Fuji.
This page was
mainly about
fact
fact
STOP
My predictions were right/wrong because . . .

A New Beak

Beauty is a bald eagle. One day, a hunter shot off half her beak. She was left with just a **stump**. So, a new beak was built for her.

First, a **model** of her beak was made. Then, the model was fitted on Beauty's beak. The model had to be **sanded** many times, because it had to fit properly.

Beauty will never be able to go back to the wild. But now that she has a new beak, she has the chance to live a long life.

Let's check: sanded

Why do you think Beauty will never be able to go back to the wild?

a stump for a beak
This page was mainly about
fact
fact
STOP
My predictions were right/wrong because . . .

Helping Oscar – A New Idea

Scientists have been working to make artificial body parts even better.

Oscar lost his two back paws in an accident. A cat cannot **survive** with just two paws. So, a doctor thought of a way to make artificial paws and attach them to Oscar's legs.

Doctors **drilled** holes into Oscar's leg bones. **Metal rods** were put into the bones. Doctors hoped that Oscar's bones and skin would grow over the metal. This **operation** was the first like it in the world.

Let's check: drilled

Why do you think doctors wanted the bones and skin to grow over the metal?

This page was mainly about
fact
fact
STOP
My predictions were right/wrong because . . .

A Success Story

Oscar's operation was a success. The idea is now being used to help people who have lost body parts.

Doctors have attached artificial body parts right into some people's bones. They have let the skin grow around the artificial part. The skin makes a tight **seal**. It helps to stop **infection** from getting in.

People and animals can now have artificial body parts that are almost as good as new.

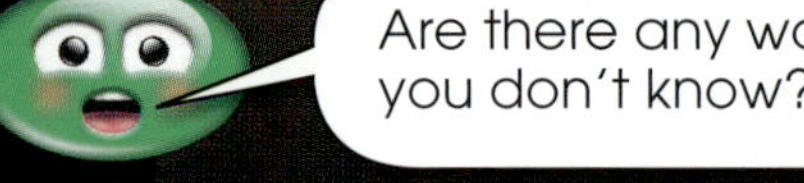

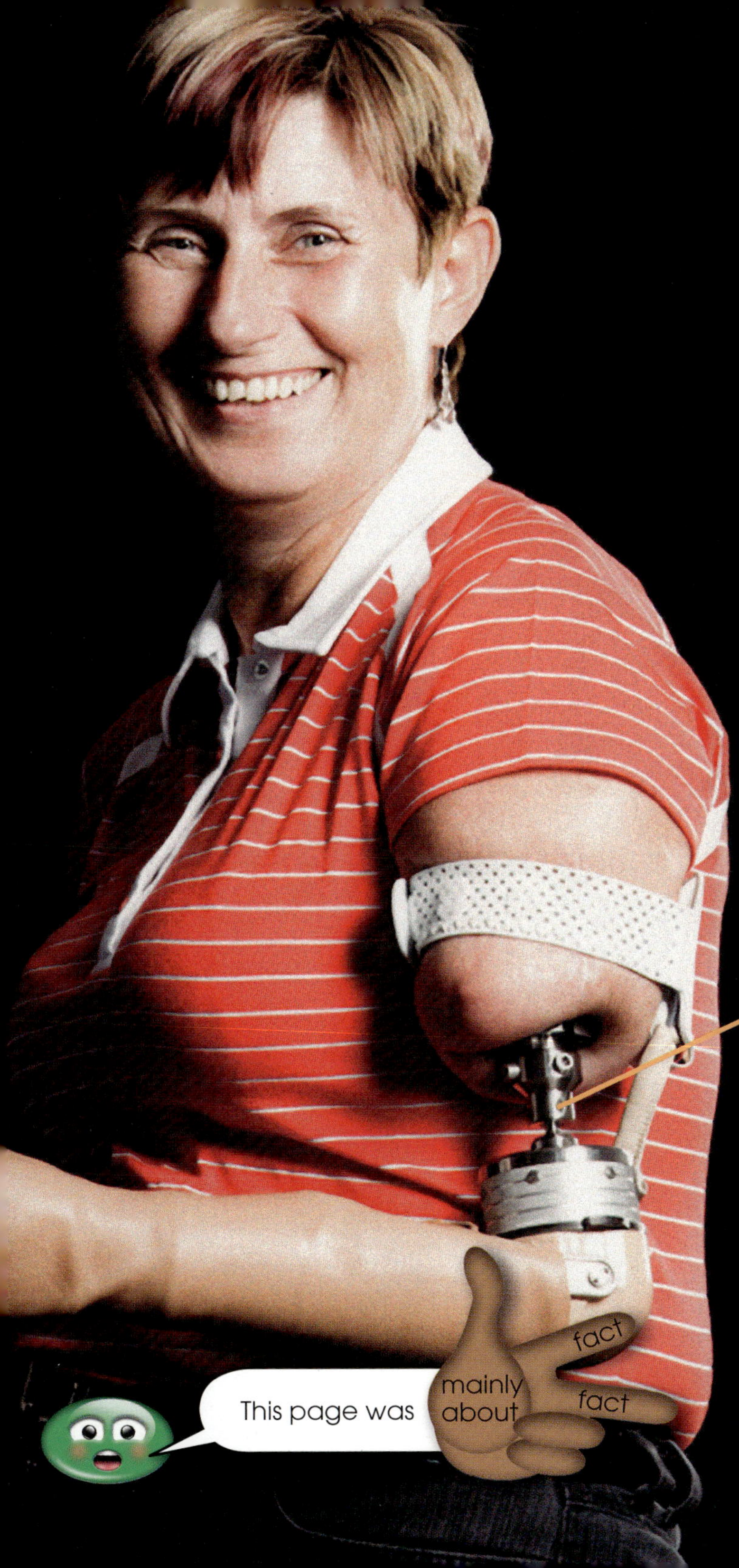

Skin has grown around the metal rod in this woman's arm. The rod is attached to her bone.

a **bionic** arm is attached to the metal rod

This page was mainly about

fact

fact

Something to Think About

 or 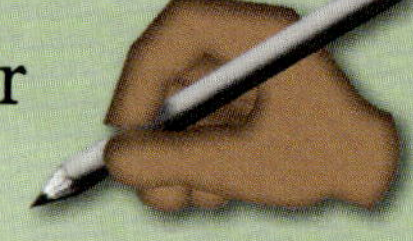

No Fin

- *Problems:*

No Beak

- *Problems:*

Think about the problems that people and animals can have when important body parts have to be removed. What can be done about these problems? Talk about your ideas with a partner, or write them down.

No _____*?*

- *Problems:*

No _____*?*

- *Problems:*

Do You Need to Find an Answer?

You could go to . . .

Library 

Expert 

Internet 

Do You Want to Find Out More?

You could look in books or on the internet using these key words to help you:

Beauty the bald eagle

Fuji the dolphin

Nadya Vessey

Oscar the bionic cat

Weta Workshop

Word Help

Dictionary

amputated	a limb taken off
artificial	made to look like something but not real
bionic	an artifical body part that is designed to replace a real body part
disease	illness
drilled	made a hole in something with a drill
infection	a disease that is caused by bacteria
metal	a hard material that melts when it is hot
model	a copy of something
operation	a treatment done by doctors to help make a person or animal healthy again
plastic	a light strong material used to make things

rods	long sticks or bars
sanded	rubbed with sandpaper to make smooth
scales	thin pieces of skin or bone that cover the outside of a fish's body
seal	a close fit
spine	a long bone down the centre of the back
stump	the part of something that is left after the main part has been removed
survive	to stay alive
wetsuit	a tight, waterproof suit that is worn in cold water and is designed to keep the body warm

Word Help

Thesaurus

answer	reply
attach	fasten, join
leap	jump, bound
part	piece
properly	correctly, right

Location Help

Where Do They Live?

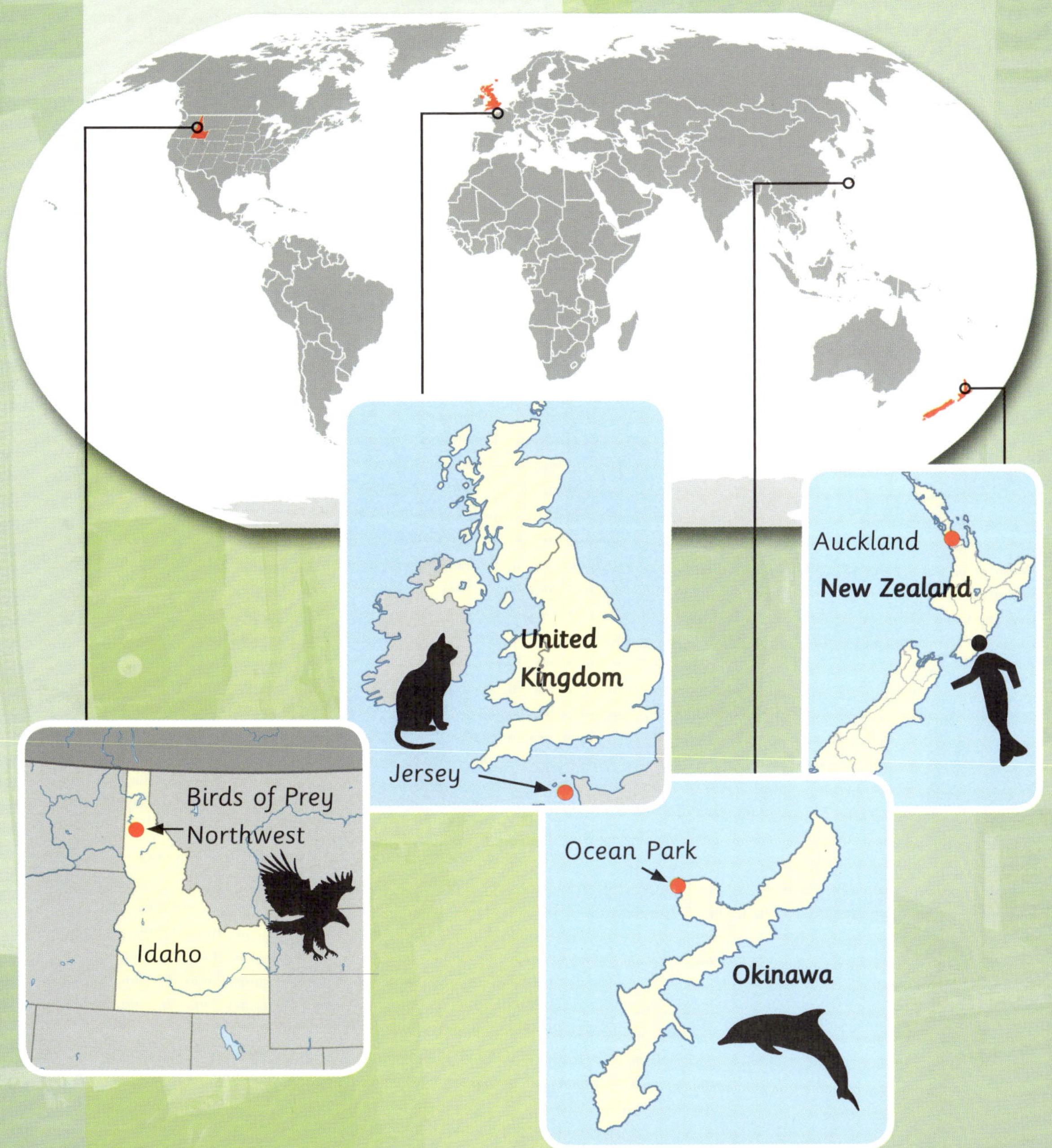

Index

amputated 4, 8

bald eagle.. 10–11

beak.. 10–11

cat.. 12–13

doctors.. 4, 12, 14

dolphin... 8–9

mermaid.. 4, 6–7

metal rods 12

model 10

tail fin...6–7, 8–9

Weta Workshop... 6–7